12 CHILDREN
WHO CHANGED THE WORLD

by Kenya McCullum

12
STORY
LIBRARY

www.12StoryLibrary.com

12-Story Library is an imprint of Peterson Publishing Company and Press Room Editions.

Produced for 12-Story Library by Red Line Editorial

Photographs ©: Anthony Behar/Sipa USA/AP Images, cover, 1, 26; Bettmann/Corbis, 4, 24, 25, 29; Dave Caulkin/AP Images, 7; John McConnico/AP Images, 8; Pavel Svoboda/ Shutterstock Images, 9; Library of Congress, 10, 15, 18, 23; The Print Collector/Corbis, 11; Detroit Publishing Company/Library of Congress, 12; Marzolino/Shutterstock Images, 13; Georgio Kollidas/Shutterstock Images, 14; Charles Dharapak/AP Images, 16; Vladimir Wrangel/Shutterstock Images, 19; Patricia Wellenbach/AP Images, 20, 28; AP Images, 21; Jaroslav Moravcik/Shutterstock Images, 22; Susan Walsh/AP Images, 27

ISBN
978-1-63235-146-3 (hardcover)
978-1-63235-187-6 (paperback)
978-1-62143-239-5 (hosted ebook)

Library of Congress Control Number: 2015934288

Printed in the United States of America
Mankato, MN
June, 2015

Go beyond the book. Get free, up-to-date content on this topic at 12StoryLibrary.com.

TABLE OF CONTENTS

RUBY BRIDGES CHALLENGES RACISM

On November 14, 1960, Ruby Bridges made history. She was the first black child to attend an all-white elementary school. Ruby was born in 1954. That year, the Supreme Court ruled schools should be desegregated. Black students could attend the same schools as white students. Before 1954, black students in Southern states often had to attend separate schools. All-black schools were often overcrowded. They did not get the same materials as students in white schools. By 1960, Ruby was ready to enter first grade in New Orleans, Louisiana. Ruby was going to make history. She was going to be the first black student at William Frantz Elementary School.

Ruby was the first black student to attend an all-white school in New Orleans, Louisiana.

On her first day, Ruby had protection from federal police officers. She needed it. As she walked to school, six-year-old Ruby was met with hatred. Crowds of people shouted racial slurs at her. Some even threatened her life.

Ruby made it into the school. But she was the only student in her class. Many white parents were angry. They did not want their children to be in class with a black student. They took their children out of school. Ruby spent the day with her teacher, Barbara Henry. For the entire year, Ruby was Henry's only student. By the end of the summer, though, white parents had become less angry. They allowed their children to go back to school. In second grade, Ruby finally had other classmates.

As an adult, Ruby shares her story. She talks about her experiences with racism. She wrote a book about her first day of school. It is called *Through My Eyes*. She started the Ruby Bridges Foundation. It educates people about racial tolerance.

4
Number of federal police officers who walked Ruby to school.

- Ruby was the first black student to attend an all-white school in the South.
- People called her nasty names and threatened her.
- She now educates people about racism.

MS. HENRY

Barbara Henry was Ruby's first grade teacher. She grew up in Boston, Massachusetts. But she taught in Louisiana. She was the only teacher who agreed to teach a black child at Ruby's school. Henry was kind to Ruby. She made her feel comfortable. But Henry moved back to Boston after that year. Ruby's school did not invite her back to teach the next school year.

2

ANNE FRANK WRITES ABOUT HER HOLOCAUST EXPERIENCE

Millions of people around the world have read *The Diary of a Young Girl*. Anne Frank wrote it during the Holocaust. She was a teenager at the time. Many children today have learned about the Holocaust through Anne's writings.

Anne was born in Germany in 1929. Her family was Jewish. In 1933, Adolf Hitler and the Nazi Party took control of Germany. The Nazis were anti-Semitic. They blamed Jewish people for Germany's problems. Under Nazi rule, Germany's Jews were poorly treated.

The Franks decided to leave Germany. Anne's family moved to the Netherlands in 1933. They lived a normal life until 1940. That year, the Nazis invaded the Netherlands. In 1942, Anne's older sister was

LIFE IN THE SECRET ANNEX

Anne's family lived in the Secret Annex with another Jewish family. There were eight people living in the small apartment. No one could leave the apartment or go outside. Friends of Anne's father helped them. They brought them food and clothes. They also gave everyone in the Secret Annex news about the outside world.

ordered to go to a Nazi death camp. They went into hiding to remain free.

Anne's family lived in a hidden apartment behind her father's

Anne's father, Otto, holds an award honoring the sale of 1 million copies of Anne's diary.

business. They called it the Secret Annex. Anne wrote in a diary about her experiences and her feelings. Anne kept writing until the Nazis captured her family in 1944. She died in a Nazi camp a year later. She was just 15 years old. A woman who helped hide the Franks kept Anne's diary. Anne's father published it in 1947. The book is available in many languages. Middle and high school students around the world still read it.

4

Months Anne spent in a Nazi camp before her death in February 1945.

- Anne and her family fled Germany to escape the Nazis.
- While living in the Netherlands, Anne began writing in her diary.
- People continue to learn about the Holocaust from Anne's diary.

THINK ABOUT IT

A diary can include all of your private thoughts and feelings about your life. You can talk about things you can't tell anyone else. Why do you think Anne kept a diary while hiding from the Nazis?

OM PRAKASH GURJAR FIGHTS AGAINST CHILD LABOR

Om Prakash Gurjar is a children's advocate in India. In 2006, he won the International Children's Peace Prize. He was 14 years old. He was recognized for helping Indian children who are forced to work.

When Om was five years old, he was forced to work on a farm. His father owed money to the landowner. Om had to work to help pay the debt. He worked on the farm for three years. He plowed the fields, harvested crops, and took care of cattle. But he was never paid. Instead, he was regularly beaten.

After three years, a group of activists rescued him. The group was called Bachpan Bachao Andolan. It works to protect children in India. The group reunited him with his family. It helped him go to school. After being rescued, Om started speaking out against child labor. He worked to create child-friendly villages in his home state. The villages ban child labor.

He also worked to help children get their birth certificates. Birth certificates prove children's ages.

These children were forced to work in crop fields, as Om was.

5

Years old Om was when he was forced to work at a farm.

- Om was rescued by children's activists after three years of being forced to work on a farm.
- He went on to fight for children's rights.
- He won the International Children's Peace Prize when he was 14.

THE INTERNATIONAL CHILDREN'S PEACE PRIZE

The International Children's Peace Prize is awarded by KidsRights, a group in the Netherlands. The prize is given to children who work for children's rights. Winners receive a cash prize. They also get a statuette called Nkosi. It shows a child moving the world. It is named after the first International Children's Peace Prize winner, Nkosi Johnson.

They list children's parents' names. They help protect children from being taken and forced to work. In 2006, Om won the International Children's Peace Prize for his work.

Some children in India must work instead of going to school.

JOAN OF ARC LEADS AN ARMY TO VICTORY

When Joan of Arc was around 12 years old, she believed God spoke to her. God told her she had to save France. In the 1410s, France was at war with England. In 1420, England and France made a peace agreement. The king of England became the ruler of England and France. But some people believed the former French prince had a right to the throne. Joan believed God commanded her to help French Prince Charles retake the throne.

In 1428, 16-year-old Joan asked Charles for permission to help him. She asked to lead the French army to battle in the city of Orleans. At first, Charles refused. But Joan would not give up. Charles finally agreed to allow Joan to lead troops into battle. In 1429,

Joan of Arc believed God wanted her to help Prince Charles.

Joan and her troops won the battle against England.

The victory allowed Charles to become the king of France. King Charles allowed Joan to lead more battles. But in 1430, Joan was captured by English troops. The people who held Joan thought her beliefs were strange. They thought she was a witch. They put her on trial for heresy. In 1431, she was burned at the stake.

After her death, Joan was considered a hero. In 1920, Pope Benedict XV declared Joan a saint. She is the patron saint of France.

70

Number of charges against Joan during her trial for heresy.

- Joan asked permission to lead the French army into battle.
- She won the battle, and Charles became king of France.
- Joan was captured, accused of being a witch, and burned at the stake.

Joan won a battle that helped Prince Charles take the throne.

WOLFGANG AMADEUS MOZART MAKES MUSIC

Wolfgang Amadeus Mozart was born in 1756 in Salzburg, Austria. His father, Leopold, was a composer. Leopold introduced his children to music at an early age. At three years old, Wolfgang watched his older sister play the keyboard. He started copying what she was doing. He showed his musical talent.

By the time he was four, Wolfgang could play several instruments. He played the clarinet, violin, and piano. By age five, he had written his first concerto. His father recognized his talent. He helped Wolfgang write more musical pieces.

Leopold wanted to show off his talented children. He took them on a tour in 1762. Six-year-old Wolfgang traveled with his family to Munich, Germany. He played in front of royalty. They also played in Vienna, Austria; Paris, France; and London, England.

Wolfgang continued writing and performing music. At 16, he became a court musician for Prince

Wolfgang showed musical talent at an early age.

Archbishop Hieronymus Colloredo of Salzburg. Wolfgang continued writing music as an adult. Today, he is considered one of the best composers in history. People continue to perform and listen to his music today.

46
Number of concertos Wolfgang Mozart wrote.

- Wolfgang Mozart could play several instruments by the time he was four.
- He started working for the prince of Salzburg when he was 16.
- He composed many pieces of music still considered important today.

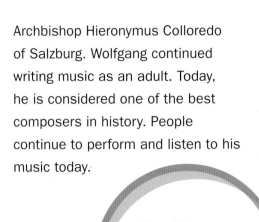

The Mozarts, including Wolfgang (center), toured Europe together.

BLAISE PASCAL MAKES WAVES IN MATHEMATICS

In the seventeenth century, Blaise Pascal was a child prodigy. He excelled in mathematics. At 16, he developed a new math theory called the mystical hexagon. Mathematicians who study geometry still consider the theory important today.

From a young age, Blaise was a talented mathematician.

Blaise was born in Clermont-Ferrand, France, in 1623. In 1631, Blaise's family moved to Paris, France. His

PASCAL'S WAGER

Blaise Pascal had ideas about religion. One of his arguments is called Pascal's Wager. It says that someone has a lot to gain or lose if God exists. So, it is best to believe in God. You have nothing to lose if you are wrong. Blaise's ideas about religion are still studied today.

50

Number of Pascalines Blaise built.

- Blaise came up with a math theory called the mystical hexagon.
- His theory impressed important mathematicians and is still studied today.
- Blaise invented an early calculator and studied religion too.

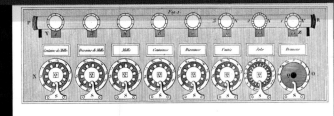

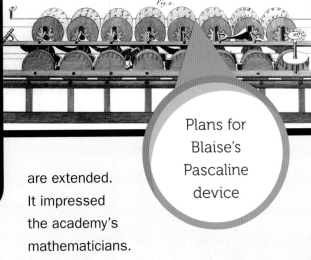

Plans for Blaise's Pascaline device

father began to teach him and his sisters at home. Blaise's father wanted him to focus on languages. He did not teach him mathematics. He did not even allow Blaise to keep a math book at home.

But this did not stop Blaise. He studied math on his own. He developed his own theories. When he was 16, Blaise's father was impressed with his work. He took Blaise to meetings at the mathematics academy in Paris. Blaise presented his theories, including his mystical hexagon theory. The theory says the sides of an irregular hexagon inside a circle meet in three points when the sides are extended. It impressed the academy's mathematicians.

Blaise continued studying math. He also began working on inventions. At 18, he developed an early version of the digital calculator. Called the Pascaline, some people consider it the first computer. He later invented the syringe and the roulette gambling wheel. These inventions are still used today.

HECTOR PIETERSON PROTESTS APARTHEID

Hector Pieterson was a 12-year-old student. He was killed while protesting apartheid in South Africa. More black people lived in South Africa than white people. But under the apartheid system, black people had to live separately from white people. They were treated poorly.

First Lady Michelle Obama (right) in front of the iconic image of Hector

WHAT WAS APARTHEID?

Apartheid was a system of laws that discriminated against black South Africans. They could not live, work, or attend school in areas where whites lived. Black people could not go in white areas without permission. Many white and black South Africans opposed apartheid. The law was finally changed in 1993.

Hector was born in 1963. At the time, schools taught students solely in the Afrikaans language. Afrikaans was the language of white South Africans. Many black South Africans felt forced to use the language of people who treated them poorly. Many teachers refused to work. Students refused to take their midterm tests.

On June 16, 1976, students in Soweto, South Africa, participated in a peaceful protest against apartheid. Though the protest was not violent, police opened fire on the crowd. Hector was one of the first students killed. A photographer took a picture of Hector after he was shot. The

400

Estimated number of students killed at the protests where Hector lost his life.

- Hector protested apartheid with other students.
- He was one of the first students police killed in the protests.
- A photograph taken of Hector after he was shot made more people aware of problems with apartheid.
- A museum was opened to honor him and remember the children who died in the protests.

photograph made him the most memorable victim. A museum was opened in Hector's honor. It was located a few blocks away from where he was killed. Hector's death brought publicity to the protest. It helped show the world the problems with apartheid.

SACAGAWEA ASSISTS LEWIS AND CLARK

Sacagawea was a member of the Shoshone people. At 16, she helped guide Meriwether Lewis and William Clark through the western United States.

Sacagawea was born in 1788 in Lemhi, Idaho. When she was 12, she was kidnapped by a Hidatsa war party. The Hidatsa people sold her to a fur trader named Toussaint Charbonneau. He took Sacagawea as one of his wives.

In November 1804, Sacagawea and Charbonneau met Lewis and Clark. They were on a trip out West. They wanted Sacagawea and Charbonneau to join them. They wanted Sacagawea to help them when they encountered Shoshone. Sacagawea spoke the tribe's

Sacagawea helped Lewis and Clark explore the western United States.

0

Number of other women in the group of 33 traveling with Lewis and Clark.

- Sacagawea helped Lewis and Clark find food.
- She worked as an interpreter between Lewis and Clark and the Shoshone.
- She was recognized for her contributions by the National American Woman Suffrage Association.

Dollar coins feature Sacagawea.

language and understood their customs. She could help Lewis and Clark speak with the Shoshone people.

Sacagawea was helpful in other ways too. She found plants and berries for the group to eat. During the trip, their boat nearly tipped over. Sacagawea saved some supplies and important documents. In 1805, Sacagawea gave birth to son Jean Baptiste Charbonneau. People who met the adventurers were friendlier because of her and her baby. She and her son made the group seem less threatening. When they met a group of Shoshone, the group leader was Sacagawea's brother. Lewis and Clark were able to buy horses they needed from the tribe.

Sacagawea has been recognized as a symbol of female strength. Her face appeared on a dollar coin in 2000. She was also recognized by the National American Woman Suffrage Association.

9
SAMANTHA SMITH WRITES TO PROMOTE PEACE

In 1982, Samantha Smith was afraid. The 10 year old lived in Maine. She read news about the possibility of war with the Soviet Union. She was so concerned that she wrote a letter to the Soviet Union's leader. She asked Yuri Andropov if he wanted to start a war with the United States. She did not think she would get a response.

But her letter made an impression with the Soviet people. It was published in the Soviet newspaper *Pravda*. In April 1983, Andropov replied to her letter. He told her he did not want war with other countries. He said Samantha was courageous and honest. He invited her to visit the Soviet Union. In July 1983, Samantha and her family went to the Soviet Union for two weeks. They toured the country. Samantha met many Soviet children who were also afraid of a war starting.

When Samantha returned to the United States, many people wanted to speak to her. She went on TV to talk about her letter and her trip. Samantha went to Japan to talk to children about peace. She wrote a book about her experiences called

Samantha with the letter she wrote to Andropov

Samantha answers questions at a press conference in Moscow.

Journey to the Soviet Union. In 1985, when she was 13 years old, Samantha died in a plane crash with her father. But Samantha's name continued to work for peace. Her mother created the Samantha Smith Foundation. The foundation started a student exchange program between the United States and the Soviet Union.

THINK ABOUT IT

Do you read or watch the news? Is there anything happening in the world right now that scares you? Why? What could you do about it?

5
Grade Samantha was in when she wrote her letter to Andropov.

- Samantha wrote a letter to Soviet leader Andropov asking if he was going to start a war with the United States.
- She traveled to the Soviet Union and met many leaders and children who were concerned about war.
- She became a peace activist and wrote a book about her life and beliefs.

YOUNG TUTANKHAMUN LEADS EGYPT

Tutankhamun was an Egyptian king. He took the throne when he was only nine years old. His rule did not last long. But he left behind priceless items. They helped scientists and historians understand more about ancient Egypt.

Tutankhamun, also known as King Tut, was born around 1341 BCE. He was in power for eight or nine years before he died. Scientists are still working to understand why he died. Since he was such a young ruler, historians believe Tutankhamun had advisors. They helped him make important decisions.

Little is known about Tutankhamun's time as king. But historians know he made a few big decisions. He moved Egypt's capital to the city of Thebes. He ordered Egyptians to stop worshipping a god called Aten.

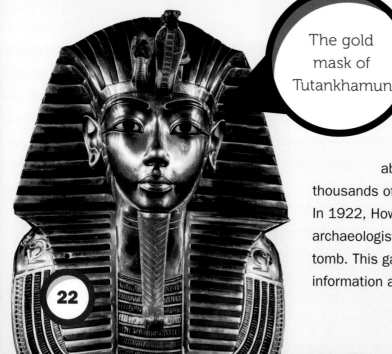

The gold mask of Tutankhamun

People did not learn more about King Tut until thousands of years after his death. In 1922, Howard Carter, a British archaeologist, found Tutankhamun's tomb. This gave the world more information about Tutankhamun.

Treasures from Tutankhamun's tomb after its discovery

Artifacts in the tomb showed what he looked like. King Tut's tomb had his mummy. It had many priceless items that tell what his life was like. They included a gold mask of King Tut, a throne, and decorated figurines. Scientists and historians have learned a lot about ancient Egypt from King Tut's tomb.

3,245

Number of years between Tutankhamun's death and Carter's discovery of his tomb.

- Tutankhamun became king of ancient Egypt when he was nine years old.
- He died after ruling for eight or nine years.
- His tomb gave scientists a better understanding of his rule and life in ancient Egypt.

KING TUT'S TOMB

Tutankhamun's tomb contained many treasures. It had oils, gold and ebony statues, jewelry, and paintings. There were even toys King Tut played with as a child. The tomb also had a solid gold coffin where Tutankhamun's mummy was found. The mummy was wrapped in linen. It had a golden mask on its face.

RYAN WHITE CHANGES HOW PEOPLE THINK ABOUT AIDS

Ryan White was a teenager from Indiana. He helped change the way people think about those who have AIDS. AIDS is a serious illness that affects the body's immune system. When he was 13 years old, Ryan contracted AIDS from a treatment for hemophilia. Hemophilia is a disease that affects the blood. It makes someone's body bleed for a long time after an injury.

Ryan helped change the way the world treated people with AIDS.

Ryan was one of the first children to get AIDS. It was the 1980s. AIDS was a new disease. People did not know a lot about it. Some people were afraid of Ryan. They believed they could catch AIDS from attending school with him. He was suspended from his school in Kokomo, Indiana, and was bullied.

Ryan and his parents sued for him to be allowed back at school. The case made the news around the United States. People became more

24

At one point, Ryan took classes over the phone.

educated about AIDS. Ryan won his case. He was allowed to go back to school. But he was still badly treated by his classmates. His parents were badly treated by people in their town.

His family moved to Cicero, Indiana, in 1987. Ryan started going to school there. He was accepted by his new classmates. They had been given information about AIDS. They knew they did not have to be afraid of Ryan.

In 1990, Ryan died from AIDS. Shortly after his death, Congress passed the Ryan White Comprehensive AIDS Resources Emergency (CARE) Act. The law helps people with the disease get the treatment they need.

4

Number of times Congress has renewed funding for the CARE Act since it became law in 1990.

- Ryan was one of the first children to get AIDS.
- He was suspended from school because of his condition.
- His story led to more AIDS education and help for AIDS patients.

MALALA YOUSAFZAI FIGHTS FOR GIRLS' EDUCATION

Malala Yousafzai is an advocate for girls' education. Malala went to school in Pakistan in the 2000s. It was dangerous for girls to go to school. Malala continued to attend school, even though her life was at risk.

Malala was born on July 12, 1997, in Mingora, Pakistan. Her father, Ziauddin, supported education for girls. He founded a school. A terrorist group called the Taliban did not want girls to be educated. They started attacking girls' schools where she lived. In response, Malala started writing about why girls should be able to go to school. This angered the Taliban. They threatened to kill her.

On October 9, 2012, a Taliban member boarded Malala's school bus. He was looking for her. He shot her in the left side of her head. He also shot two of her friends. Malala survived the attack after treatment at two different hospitals. Her friends also survived the attack.

Malala fully recovered from her injuries. She continued to speak in support for girls' education. She has been praised for her bravery and her work helping

Malala stood up for educating girls.

14

Years old Malala was when she was shot by the Taliban.

- Malala wrote about the need to educate girls in Pakistan.
- Her writing angered members of the Taliban, who attempted to kill her.
- She has been praised around the world for her bravery and dedication to girls' education.

girls get an education. In 2014, she became the youngest person to win the Nobel Peace Prize. A year before,

THINK ABOUT IT

How important is education to you? Would you risk your life for an education? If someone threatened you for going to school, would you still want to go? Why or why not?

Malala won the Sakharov prize for Freedom of Thought. She also won Pakistan's National Youth Peace Prize in 2011. Malala has written a book about her life. It is called *I Am Malala: The Girl Who Stood Up for Education and Was Shot by the Taliban*. She started the Malala Fund to help young girls around the world get an education.

Malala speaks at a Malala Fund event on the International Day of the Girl in 2013.

malalafund.org

HOW YOU CAN MAKE CHANGE

Speak Up

If there is something you care about, write letters to tell adults about it. Write to government officials, newspapers, and business leaders and ask them for help. Talk about your concerns in person. Often, adults listen when kids speak up.

Volunteer

Give your time volunteering for a cause you care about. There are many organizations that need your help. Ask an adult to go with you to an animal shelter, soup kitchen, library, museum, or other organization that relies on volunteers.

Sign a Petition

Is there something you would like to change at school or in your neighborhood? If so, write a petition to your principal or local government. Petitions are written requests for change. Many people may sign a single petition. Gather as many signatures as you can to show your idea is supported by the community.

GLOSSARY

activists
People who actively work for political or social change.

advocate
Someone who supports a cause.

anti-Semitic
Hating Jewish people.

archaeologist
Someone who studies ancient peoples and cultures.

child labor
The use of children for work in business, agriculture, or industry.

concerto
A piece of music for one or more instruments with an orchestra.

desegregated
End of policies that keep different races apart.

heresy
Beliefs that are different from the official beliefs of a particular religion.

Holocaust
The killing of millions of Jewish and other people by the Nazis during World War II (1939–1945).

racial slur
An insulting remark regarding race.

racism
The belief that some races are superior to others.

terrorist
Someone who uses violence to scare people, often to achieve a political goal.

tomb
A building above or below the ground where a dead body is kept.

FOR MORE INFORMATION

Books

McCann, Michelle Roehm. *Boys Who Rocked the World*. New York: Aladdin, 2012.

McCann, Michelle Roehm. *Girls Who Rocked the World*. New York: Aladdin, 2012.

Yousafzai, Malala. *I Am Malala: How One Girl Stood Up for Education and Changed the World*. New York: Little, Brown, 2014.

Websites

Children's Museum: Power of Children
www.childrensmuseum.org/exhibits/power-of-children

Kids Make a Difference
www.scholastic.com/browse/collection.jsp?id=504

Volunteering: How Can I Make a Difference?
www.pbskids.org/itsmylife/emotions/volunteering/article3.html

INDEX

About the Author

Kenya McCullum is a writer who
lives in California. When she is not
working, she enjoys spending time
with friends and family, going to the
beach, and volunteering for causes
she believes in.

READ MORE FROM 12-STORY LIBRARY

Every 12-Story Library book
is available in many formats,
including Amazon Kindle
and Apple iBooks. For more
information, visit your device's
store or 12StoryLibrary.com.